Purely Single

by
Kathleen Ruth Senat

Copyright Notice

**Kathleen Ruth Senat
Purely-Single**

© 2014, Kathleen Ruth Senat
Anointed Fire™ Christian Book Publishing
katsenat@live.com

Unless otherwise indicated, scripture
quotations in this book are taken from The King
James Bible.

ISBN-13:
978-0692286661 (Anointed Fire)

ISBN-10:
0692286667

Dedication

This book is dedicated to my FATHER. YOU gave me the vision, and now, YOU have provided a means for it to be fulfilled.

This book is also dedicated to all who need to be set free from sexual sin and/ or toxic relationships, or the tendency to be involved in either. I pray this book gives you hope that it's never too late to do things GOD'S way.

Acknowledgments

I would like to acknowledge the following people for their contributions, support, and prayers. First and foremost, this book would not be possible without revelation from GOD.

Then there are my pastors: Pastor Charles Turner III and Pastor Marilyn Turner who have encouraged and prayed for me. I acknowledge Tiffany Kameni for believing in me and mentoring me. I thank Roserbie Theoc, Roberta Theoc, Sharmica Theoc-Paul, Vicky Destine, Michelet Paul, Diana Charles, Schella Jean, Rabson Senat, Nathalie Salazar, Steve Hogge, Joanne Petite, Ed-Lyne Metayer, Purrel Miller, Tania Montanez, Anna Johnson, Susan Kennedy, Christina Neptune, Davinia Gordon, Sophonie Joseph, Martine Aurelus, Danette Ruiz and all my Purely Single blog supporters for believing in me, supporting me, praying for me and being there. Just a simple good job goes such a long way, and I am so thankful for your encouragement.

Introduction

In this book, you will learn in detail what it means to be purely single and how to live a purely single lifestyle. I will address worldly misconceptions that prevent believers from walking in purity. In addition, you will learn about the obstacles to purely single living, as well as how to overcome them. I will also explain the effects of living an impure life, and why purely single living is best for anyone who is unmarried. You will learn to be content in your singleness while preparing for a Godly marriage.

The content of this book is based on revelation given to me by the Holy Spirit, what the WORD of GOD says on the subject, and my own personal experience.

Table of Contents

Chapter 1

Purely Single Movement

What Does it Mean to be Purely Single?

Purely Single is not just a title, but it is a movement based on the following scripture:

1 Thessalonians 4:3-4 KJV
For this is the will of God, even your sanctification, that ye should abstain from fornication: That every one of you should know how to possess his vessel in sanctification and honour.

In other words, honor your body in the LORD.

To be purely single means to be abstinent until marriage, and to wait on GOD for your spouse. This means a single person takes precautionary measures to ensure that there is no sexual activity prior to marriage, including masturbation. The single also makes a

1

decision to wait on the one person GOD has as their mate, and will not date any random person for the sake of dating. Marriage should always be the goal when pursuing romantic relationships. Therefore, a purely single individual does not willingly entertain counterfeits.

A counterfeit is a person who looks like the husband or wife ordained by GOD but is not. Counterfeits are sent as distractions to keep you outside of GOD'S will. They are not to be taken lightly, and should be handled with caution. They must be kept at a distance or eliminated from a single's circle (if possible). Look at it this way: If the person was not sent by GOD, then he or she is on an assignment given by the enemy. So, if you're desiring to be purely single, you should keep in mind that the enemy has a way of causing us to go further into sin than we intended to go. What may start off as a harmless conversation may lead to the development of a toxic relationship. You may not have planned for a relationship to develop but end up in one anyhow. Therefore, it is wise to not take any chances with the enemy, and you do this by promptly placing a counterfeit in his or her proper place.

Being single may or may not be a choice, but living purely single is always intentional. In addition to making conscious decisions to remain purely single, you must also be proactive in maintaining your purity. Some safety precautions may seem over the top, but the WORD teaches us to flee from fornication. This means that staying away from sin is not enough. A purely single individual takes every necessary step to prevent circumstances that may potentially lead to sin. Therefore, you are purely single when:

- You are single and make seeking GOD your priority over everything else, including seeking a mate.
- You desire to use this time of singleness to go deeper in Him with no ulterior motives, only to get to know Him better.
- You choose singleness over being with a mate who you know displeases GOD.

- You refuse to entertain counterfeits... period.
- You allow GOD to choose the one He has for you.
- You are abstinent while waiting on marriage. This includes refraining from masturbation.
- You allow GOD to prepare you for marriage by allowing Him to mold you into the wife (or husband) who honors GOD.

Who Should Be Purely Single?

To live purely single is the will of GOD. Anyone who is single should follow the guidelines of being purely single. However, there are certain groups of people who tend to believe that they are not expected to live this lifestyle. These people are usually divorced, widowed, and single parents.

The WORD of GOD is clear. Sex is reserved for a man and a woman who are married to each other. Anything outside of that is displeasing to GOD. The following scripture supports this:

Romans 8:5-9 KJV
For they that are after the flesh do mind the things of the flesh; but they that are after the Spirit the things of the Spirit. For to be carnally minded is death; but to be spiritually minded is life and peace. Because the carnal mind is enmity against God: for it is not subject to the law of God, neither indeed can be. So then they that are in the flesh cannot please God. But ye are not in the flesh, but in the Spirit, if so be that the Spirit of God dwell in you. Now if any man have not the Spirit of Christ, he is none of his.

1 Corinthians 6:9 KJV
Know ye not that the unrighteous shall not inherit the kingdom of God? Be not deceived: neither fornicators, nor idolaters, nor adulterers, nor effeminate, nor abusers of themselves with mankind.....

Even after knowing what the Bible says, many people feel that they are an exception, especially many who are divorced, widowed, or single parents. The reasons many people feel that living a purely single life is not for them is because they feel it's silly or unrealistic. They tend to view it as a standard for the inexperienced, such as teens and young adults. However, this is not true. GOD does not honor sex outside of marriage, regardless of past experiences, age, background, gender, or for any reason. Also bear in mind that righteousness is not the norm. The world we live in is not righteous, so resistance to righteous living is to be expected. To the world, purely single living is unrealistic, and for that reason, they reject the lifestyle.

1 Corinthians 2:14 KJV
But the natural man receiveth not the things of the Spirit of God: for they are foolishness unto him: neither can he know them, because they are spiritually discerned.

In summary, anyone who is single should live purely single. A person should not use the fact that purity is unpopular in the world as a means to determine if it's doable. Just because it seems as if everyone is dating freely and participating in fornication doesn't mean it's impossible to live according to purely single standards. As a matter of fact, my motto for this movement is: *Purity is not extinct...and far from impossible.* In other words, it may be an unpopular lifestyle, but there are people living it, and this means it's possible.

Why Purely Single Living?

Now that we've established what it means to live purely single and who should live it, we can explore the reasons purity is essential. Some reasons for living purely single are:

- Purity pleases GOD.
- Purity protects our bodies.
- Purity protects our hearts.

Living purely single is pleasing to GOD. According to 1 Corinthians 6:9, fornicators and adulterers are listed amongst the people who will not inherit the Kingdom of Heaven. This covers the first part of pure singleness, which is to be abstinent until marriage. The second part of pure singleness deals with trusting GOD enough to guide you. It pleases HIM to know you trust HIM with your life, instead of trying to do things your own way.

Living purely single protects our bodies from some unfortunate circumstances. There are so many people walking around with sexually transmitted diseases and infections, and many are completely unaware they have them. There are also people who know they are infected; nevertheless, they intentionally infect others as a means of getting revenge. Engaging in sex puts your body at risk of contracting sexually transmitted diseases. Remember, you won't always know who is infected.

Sexually transmitted diseases are not to be taken lightly. There are some diseases that can be cured, while there are others with no known cure. There are both curable and incurable diseases that can cause infertility and possibly death. Some people contract multiple sexually transmitted diseases at a time. Unfortunately, contracting an STD is more common than we'd like to believe, but GOD protects us by giving us guidelines on how to live. Abstinence protects us from STDs; all the same, GOD will not send someone to infect you. It is essential to wait on HIM to send you a disease-free spouse.

In addition to protecting our bodies, purely single living protects our hearts. When we choose to give our bodies to engage in premarital sex, there are consequences to expect. A child can be conceived. A child born out of wedlock is likely to be unwanted by one or both parents. While every situation is different, the most common scenario is one where the mother wants the child, but the father doesn't. This brings about feelings of rejection and can seriously damage the mother's (and child's) self esteem. Oftentimes, this is when the relationship ends or is at its breaking point. Whatever the scenario, someone walks away hurt.

Another tragedy that can result from unwanted pregnancies is abortion. Abortion is so common that people have become desensitized to it. It has become another form of birth control, and has even been embraced by some churches. More often than not, a woman facing an unwanted pregnancy will have an abortion or at least consider one. This is true, even if she is pro-life. The burden of possibly raising a child without support from the father or the risk of losing the father seems to overwhelm her to the point of making decisions that are out of character for her.

Abortions can be a health risk. There are women who find themselves unable to have children because of some internal damage sustained during an abortion procedure. There have been reports of tissue and other things being left behind that have caused infections. Also, there is always the health risk involved in using anesthesia.

In addition to being a physical risk to a woman's body, abortion affects her emotionally. She has to live with the guilt of "getting rid" of her baby, and wondering what the child's life would have been like. She may be plagued with thoughts that she will probably never conceive when she is ready to have a child. She may also deal with condemnation. She may think that GOD is angry with her, and she isn't worthy of HIS forgiveness. Those thoughts can distance her from GOD during those times when she really needs to be drawing closer to HIM to heal.

I have personally been there. I had my first abortion when I was 18 years old. The father and I decided that we were too young to endure the responsibility of raising a child. When my mother found out that I was pregnant, she also insisted that I have an abortion. When the procedure was finished, I felt guilty, but I didn't feel too guilty because I was in the world. I wondered if I would be able to have a child whenever I was ready, and those thoughts bothered me. I had friends who'd had abortions, and one of my friends in particular had many miscarriages. These miscarriages were possibly the results of having abortions. So, I was afraid that this would be my fate.

About five years later, I found myself pregnant again. I thought I was given another chance, but from as early as four weeks, I began having complications. After agonizing weeks of testing, I found out I had an ectopic pregnancy. This means the fetus was not in place, and would not develop properly. For weeks, they didn't find a heartbeat, and I eventually had to have the deceased child removed. I was devastated and blamed myself for the destruction of my second pregnancy.

Two years later, I got pregnant again. I spent my entire pregnancy in fear of every possible thing that could go wrong. I was not sure if GOD had forgiven me for my abortion, so I expected to be punished. However, I gave birth to my beautiful son in 2008.

The following year, I got pregnant again. I had left my son's father when he was seven months old and had a new boyfriend, and he did not want the child. Once again, I had an abortion.

This time was difficult emotionally. I was afraid to pray because I didn't feel worthy to speak to GOD. I was in the world, but I was sin conscious because I was afraid to ask for forgiveness. I knew that if I got pregnant again and wasn't ready, I would abort the child again, even though I knew I would feel terrible after the fact.

Several months later, I found myself pregnant again, and I was devastated. The relationship had already gone sour, and the last thing I wanted was to have his baby. Nevertheless, I did not want to endure another abortion. Despite it all, the father of my child insisted that we weren't ready. I resisted the idea of having an abortion but eventually agreed that it would be for the best. I really didn't want to terminate my pregnancy. I felt I was risking every chance of ever having children again, but I wasn't ready to be a single mother of two children either.

GOD had a different plan. We were never able to come up with the money. Something always came up. When I was almost four months pregnant, I came to terms with the idea that I was having a second child. Two months later, I gave birth to my daughter. She was severely premature, weighing one pound and seven ounces. She had other complications, such as bleeding in her brain, and that caused me to feel really guilty for my previous abortions. Her condition made me feel horrible about almost aborting her. I blamed myself for her suffering. I became depressed and did not want to live.

GOD took this time of sorrow and worked it out for my good. My daughter's medical condition got worse, and her dad was nowhere to be found. I had some really loyal friends who came around and showed their support, but I still felt lonely. This led me to church and then to CHRIST. Needless to say, I needed GOD, but there was something else I needed. I needed to heal and receive HIS forgiveness for those abortions and other sins. I walked around for years feeling condemnation. I needed to accept CHRIST so HE could free me from the shame I felt, and I needed to understand that I was already forgiven. My heart was shattered and in need of healing.

There are other ways purely single living can protect your heart. Since you can't see the heart of man, you can be misled. Because of this, you risk opening yourself up to being hurt by choosing someone who is not right for you. The person can be unfaithful, abusive, disrespectful, and have many other ungodly characteristics. When they reveal their true nature, you can end up getting hurt. However, when you allow GOD to choose your mate, you get the PERFECT one for you. The person will have imperfections, but your partner will be what you want and everything you need. GOD will not send anyone HE cannot trust to protect your heart. HE will not send you someone who is unfaithful, abusive, infected with a sexually transmitted disease or infection, or anyone HE knows will harm you. Waiting on GOD to choose your future spouse protects your heart, body, and soul.

To live purely single means to abstain from sex

until marriage and to wait on GOD to send your mate. Anyone who is single should live this lifestyle to protect his or her heart and body. Most importantly, a person should do it to please GOD.

Chapter 2

Obstacles

In the previous chapter, we talked about why choosing the purely single lifestyle is the right choice. There are numerous obstacles that may come in the way of being purely single. The first step to overcoming them is to accept being single and to not perceive it as some kind of plague to get rid of. In a later chapter, I will discuss things to do while waiting for marriage, but in the meantime, your mindset about being single has to be a positive one.

There is nothing wrong with desiring to be married. In fact, there are very few people called to singleness, and those who are usually know that they are. Therefore, it is safe to assume that it is GOD'S will for you to marry. So, do not apologize for desiring marriage, but learn to appreciate your season of singleness as well. This does not mean to give up all hope of getting married. GOD prolongs the blessing when we are not ready to receive it because HE knows that receiving our mates prematurely will do more harm than good. HE prepares us so that we can be in the right place spiritually and emotionally to receive and properly care for that blessing. Now, accept that your desire for marriage is HIS will, but it hasn't happened yet because it's not your season. This makes the wait for marriage less difficult.

Once you understand that GOD will give you the desires of your heart in HIS timing, learn to be content with your present situation. HE wants you to be content in HIM. Your desires should not outweigh serving HIM. GOD wants you in a place where, even if you don't get your heart's desires, being in HIM is more than enough for you. In other words, getting married should not become your god.

Matthew 6:33 KJV
But seek ye first the kingdom of God, and his righteousness; and all these things

shall be added unto you.

GOD wants to be first. Once you have HIM in HIS proper position, HE can mold you into someone HE can trust to take care of the blessings HE bestows upon you. HE can also trust you to not forsake HIM once you receive your blessings. Seeking HIM and HIS righteousness also gives HIM access to your mind to transform your way of thinking. HE wants you to desire to please HIM above all things. When this happens, your desires begin to line up with HIS WORD and HIS will. Therefore, you will begin to pray HIS will for your life, and that's when HE can add your heart's desires unto you. This is how it has to happen because we oftentimes don't know what is good for us and therefore, desire things that would eventually destroy us. HE knows all things and wants to protect us from any harm that we may be unable to foresee.

Psalms 37:4 KJV
Delight thyself also in the Lord; and he
shall give thee the desires of thine heart.

When you delight in the LORD, you come into agreement with HIS will for your life. Therefore, giving you your heart's desires aligns with HIS will.

You are single because GOD wants you that way until HE determines it's time to change your relationship status. Understanding HIS will for you to be single (for now) plays an essential role in overcoming the obstacles of single living.

Being purely single can be quite challenging. If you're unaware of GOD'S will, struggle with rebellion, or continue to fall into temptation, you may find it difficult to be purely single.

Unaware of GOD'S Will

If you are unaware of the fact that GOD wants you single, you will not be able to be purely single, or at least, not intentionally. This is because you will be constantly trying to change your relationship status before being ready for that change. Remember, the second part to living purely singleness is waiting on your

GOD-ordained mate. GOD may be saying that it is not your time yet; meanwhile, you are out somewhere pursuing relationships. This is how being unaware of GOD'S will can be an obstacle to living a purely single lifestyle.

Being in a relationship before its time, even with the right person, is as harmful as being with a counterfeit. Remember, a counterfeit is someone who looks like your GOD-ordained mate but is not. Additionally, if the person is not sent by GOD, he or she is on assignment for the enemy. So, choosing your own timing instead of GOD'S timing has the same consequences as choosing your own mate instead of the one GOD ordained for you. GOD won't bless what HE didn't approve. If there is no blessing, there is no covering, and the enemy (the devil) has rights to that relationship. Once the enemy gains access, he will try to destroy you. He will come in and try to keep you outside of GOD'S will. He'll try to seduce you into sexual immorality, and if he can't get to you, he'll try to create strife between you and your partner. There are so many ways the devil can enter a relationship and bring havoc on that relationship, and they include: infidelity, domestic violence, and so many other issues. What's worse is the fact that he oftentimes goes completely unnoticed, and this is extremely dangerous.

Remember, if GOD wants you single at the moment, everyone is a counterfeit. So no matter how saved a person is or how great that person seems, you are outside of GOD'S will if you pursue that relationship. This is how being unaware of GOD'S plan stands in the way of being purely single, because you're not waiting on GOD if you're dating out of season.

Rebellious

Being unaware of GOD'S will is one obstacle to being purely single, but being rebellious makes it more challenging. When you are unaware of GOD'S will, your disobedience is unintentional. Rebellion adds to the offense, since rebellion itself is sin. To be rebellious against GOD means you know what HE expects of you, but you willingly choose not to do it.

If you are rebellious, you will not end a relationship you know is outside of GOD'S will. As mentioned earlier, once GOD is out of a relationship, the devil has rights to it. Therefore, this makes it easier to commit fornication, adultery, or participate in anything displeasing to GOD. A rebellious mindset makes it impossible to intentionally live purely single.

Constantly Falling

Another obstacle that may prevent you from being purely single is constant backsliding. You may have made up your mind to do things GOD'S way but struggle with following through with your plans. If you don't take the time to draw closer to GOD and study HIS WORD, the devil can come in with his lies and make you feel condemnation. All he wants is to make you believe you can't do it so you can give up.

Please know that GOD will forgive you if you mess up. Just understand that the flesh doesn't desire a purely single lifestyle. The flesh wants to have sex whenever it wants, and it doesn't want to wait for the GOD-ordained mate. That's because your flesh doesn't want to do anything that requires exercising self-control. That's why it is so hard to remain abstinent, but do not lose hope. This battle was never meant to be fought alone. You need GOD to sustain you, so surrender it all to GOD. Surrender your will, frustrations, failures, disappointments, and weaknesses over to HIM. HE will keep you, and if you lose your way and fall again, just know HE is waiting on you to get back up and continue the journey.

Mindset

Overcoming the obstacles to living a pure life boils down to your mindset. Your mindset will determine your success in walking in purity. If you feel that there is nothing wrong with having premarital sex or that it's impossible to abstain from it, you will not be able to overcome temptation, even if you try.

Romans 12:2 KJV
And be not conformed to this world: but be ye transformed by the renewing of your

mind, that ye may prove what is that good, and acceptable, and perfect, will of God.

If you think like the world, you will act like the world. Acting like the world is not pleasing to GOD; therefore, your mind will have to be renewed to help you to live in HIS will for you.

As you spend time in GOD'S presence and studying the WORD, your mind will constantly be renewed. Some of your old ways of thinking will be put aside as you come into agreement with the WORD of GOD. Some of the things you used to enjoy doing will lose their appeal to you. Your focus will be more towards pleasing GOD. Your renewed mind will indeed transform you.

It is important that you understand that to take on a CHRIST-like mindset, you need the help of the Holy Spirit. This is not something you can do on your own. Only the Holy Spirit can guide you in all truth so that you can discern the will of GOD.

Once your mind has been renewed, your right choices will follow. This is why it is essential that you study the WORD of GOD. As your mind becomes renewed, you will find that some of the things you thought you could never do are actually possible. Many of the restrictions we place on ourselves are in the mind.

For example, if you have ever tried to lose weight through a personal trainer, nutritionist, or any other weight-loss expert, you will better understand how your mindset affects your progress. A nutritionist will tell you that your stomach is actually satisfied long before you stop eating because your mind (or brain) doesn't realize you're full. This is because you're accustomed to a certain portion of food. They will also tell you that overeating causes your stomach to stretch so that you can eat whatever amount you've been taking in more easily, thus causing you to easily gain weight. Yet, if you train your mind to listen to your stomach and eat portioned meals, you'll notice your body is actually satisfied with a lot less food than your mind thought you needed.

The same holds true for exercising. If you were to do 25 jumping jacks and start to feel as if you're out of breath, you may think that 25 is all you can do. Your fitness instructor may tell you to do 75 more, and even though you believe that you can't do it, to your surprise, you'll make it through. The issue was that you told yourself you couldn't do more than 25 jumping jacks, but your instructor challenged that belief and pushed you. Once you become convinced that you can do more, you'll actually be comfortable with doing more. Once you reach 26, you'll believe for 27, and this will continue until you've completed 100 jumping jacks.

This is why I stress studying the WORD of GOD because it challenges your way of thinking and moves you to think like CHRIST. Once you come into agreement with GOD'S standards for purity and HIS plan for your life, you will act accordingly. You will make a decision to stop fornicating and dating counterfeits. Once the decision is made, HE gives you the strength to stand, and you are able to overcome temptation. The way to overcome any and every obstacle is to take on the mindset of victory over that obstacle.

Let me share my testimony with you to encourage you to believe that you can be purely single, no matter how deep in sin you think you may be in. Being purely single may seem intimidating at first, but it is not impossible.

I was once in the world and lived a life that was completely opposite of the purely single lifestyle. I couldn't stand to be alone, so I went from one relationship to the next. I didn't allow myself to heal from the previous relationship before jumping into the next one. I was also engaging in premarital sex and even lived with men on two separate occasions.

The idea of pure singleness would have been a joke to me at that time. I could not imagine waiting until marriage to have sex, and definitely could not wrap my mind around being single and content. Even though I kept getting hurt by men, I went from one bad relationship to the next. I was attracting some of the same kind of men; they were just packaged differently. Regardless of their ages, social statuses, ethnic backgrounds, or whatever characteristics they had, I kept encountering some of the same problems. I have endured infidelity, abandonment, domestic violence, and rape after trying to choose my own mate. Even after going through those horrific events, it didn't occur to me that I needed to wait on GOD. I just felt like those men were the problem and not my own lack of judgment.

Nowadays, I have refrained from dating altogether. It has been several years since I've been on a single date. I am content being single, and I refuse to date just because I feel lonely. My desire to please GOD and have HIS blessing outweighs my desire to be married. I trust GOD to send my husband when HE sees fit. I am actually too busy with ministry to be overwhelmed with feelings of loneliness. Don't get me wrong, there have been some difficult times and temptations along the way, but GOD has sustained me. HE also healed the brokenness that caused me to look to a man to validate me. I was looking to fill voids that only Jesus could fill. I thought that a relationship could make me happy, but the truth was that I needed to learn to be happy by myself in order to be happy in a relationship.

If I was able to turn away from an impure lifestyle and live purely single, anyone can. It is never too late to start. There is no such thing as being in too deep to come out. Once you make up your mind to do GOD'S will, HE will help you to do just that. You just have to understand that you can't do it in your own strength; instead, you have to depend on GOD. HE will walk you through every necessary step to get you on the path of righteousness. HE will change your mindset so that you will learn to avoid certain behaviors or situations that may cause you to stumble. Once again, if HE did it for me, HE can and will do it for you.

Also, remember the reason you decided to live

a purely single lifestyle. If you haven't been living a lifestyle of purity, you've likely chosen this route because you've realized that doing things your way wasn't working. You've likely endured some horrible consequences and decided it was time for a change. Keep these things in mind when you feel yourself falling off track.

I had to learn the hard way that my way was leading me towards destruction. I had been in and out of relationships that left me broken. It didn't occur to me that I needed to do something different until I let GOD in. I knew that doing things my way would mean more pain, so I decided to allow GOD to lead me.

Identify what your obstacles are and be honest with yourself. Once you recognize what's standing in the way of living purely single, you can take the necessary steps to overcome them. Keep in mind that you are not alone. Your help comes from GOD.

I conducted a survey to get a better view of the

mindsets people have towards purity and dating. The participants were between the ages of 25 and 40, both male and female, single and married, and Christian and non-Christian. I was aiming to cover a broader demographic and chose not to limit my survey to Christians alone. Here are the questions I asked eight people:

1. Do you believe it's possible for people to wait until marriage to have sex if they have already engaged in sex before?

2. Do you think passionate kissing is okay before marriage? Please support your answer.

3. Do you think it's possible for two people who've already engaged in premarital sex with each other to stop and wait until marriage?

4. Do you think it's impractical for single parents to decide to wait until marriage to have sex?

5. Do you think it's possible for a single mother to expect to meet a GOD fearing man who will love her children, wait until marriage to have sex, and who actually wants to marry her? Please support your answer.

6. How long should it take two people in a relationship to realize they want to marry each other? How long is too long?

7. Do you believe that GOD chooses or even cares who we marry? Please support your answer.

Results

1. Do you believe it's possible for people to wait until marriage to have sex if they have already engaged in sex before?

Results: Everyone answered yes. They all believed that if the two parties agree, then abstinence is possible.

2. Do you think passionate kissing is okay before marriage? Please support your

answer.

Results: Six said no to passionate kissing, but the other two didn't see it as a problem.

3. Do you think it's possible for two people who've already engaged in premarital sex with each other to stop and wait until marriage?

Results: Every participant unanimously said yes. Three believed it would be difficult for two people who had already been intimate with each other to stop, but believed that anything is possible with GOD.

4. Do you think it's impractical for single parents to decide to wait until marriage to have sex?

Results: Every participant said no. They believed that single parents can wait until marriage to have sex.

5. Do you think it's possible for a single mother to expect to meet a GOD fearing man who will love her children, wait until marriage to have sex, and who actually

wants to marry her? Please support your answer.

Results: Every participant said yes. They all believed that GOD will send a husband who is willing to wait and who will view the single mother as his blessing.

6. How long should it take two people in a relationship to realize they want to marry each other? How long is too long?

Results: One out of the eight said the couple should know right away whether or not they wanted to be married. Two out of eight said six months to a year. Two out of eight said three or more years was acceptable. Three out of the eight said time was irrelevant.

7. Do you believe that GOD chooses or even cares who we marry? Please support your answer.

Results: Everyone believed GOD chooses our mates and cares who we marry.

Chapter 3

Let's Do It

Now that you know what it means to live purely single, why it is necessary, and some of the obstacles that get in the way of living it, you're ready to start living it.

Make a Decision

First, make up your mind and decide what lifestyle you really want. Do you truly want to live purely single? Carefully weigh the pros and cons to make sure you're willing to make the necessary sacrifices, and then take action.

Think of it like making a decision to lose weight. You've made up your mind, and you really want to lose weight. Therefore, you must understand that sacrifices have to be made to achieve this goal. You will have to give up certain foods and push yourself to be physically active. Then go ahead and do those things that will give you the results you desire.

In the same manner, make a decision to live according to purely single standards. Consider the cost. You'll probably have to limit some social interactions, sever ties with certain people, and maybe avoid certain environments altogether.

Pray

No one can successfully fulfill a commitment of purity in their own strength. This is where prayer is necessary.

James 5:16 KJV
Confess your faults one to another, and pray one for another, that ye may be healed. The effectual fervent prayer of a righteous man availeth much.

The way to pray an effectual fervent prayer is for you to feel passionate about the thing you are praying about. When you allow the Holy Spirit to come in and renew your mind so that you desire GOD'S will, you will become passionate about pleasing GOD. You can be sure that GOD is in agreement with your prayer, and it will be answered.

Therefore, if you desire to be purely single because you want to please GOD, you can be. HE will hold your hand during the journey and keep you on the right path. If you have other selfish or ulterior motives, you will definitely fall into temptation because anytime GOD is not your motivation, you'll find yourself trying to sustain yourself. You cannot sustain yourself because the flesh wants to satisfy itself. Only GOD is able to sustain you. HE is also willing.

Pray so that you can accurately discern the will of GOD. He will also put the desire in you to do HIS will, and this desire leads to the strength to follow through and do HIS will. This is how the effectual prayer of the righteous availeth much.

Let Go

In order to live in purity, there are some things you will have to let go of. When you spend time in prayer, GOD will reveal things to you. HE'LL show you your heart, and when you're ready, HE'LL show you the things that need to be removed. The best way to cooperate is to let go of anything HE'S trying to remove from you. You may have to let go of certain mindsets, friends, your current relationship, social interactions, and so many other things.

Your mind needs to be renewed so you can have a CHRIST-like mindset. In order for this to be effective, your old ways of thinking must be discarded. You can't have both CHRIST-like thinking and worldly thinking because they contradict each other. The old way of thinking has to be removed to make room for the new way of thinking. Both mindsets cannot dwell in you. If you think premarital sex is okay or impossible to avoid, being single is a punishment, it's okay to give any man a chance, seeking revenge, or acting on emotions is okay, your mind needs to be renewed. These mindsets have to be removed in order for your mind to be renewed.

If you come into agreement with GOD'S

WORD concerning premarital sex, then you will refrain from premarital sex. Premarital sex is sin before GOD, and is therefore forbidden. Anything that GOD forbids is for your own protection. It can either cause physical harm, emotional distress, or cause you to distance yourself from HIM. Distancing yourself from GOD gives the devil easier access to you. When the devil gets in, your spiritual well-being is threatened.

In order to live purely single, you must do away with any notion that premarital sex is okay or that it's impossible to avoid. You cannot practice abstinence if you don't agree with it or believe it's possible. When you remove this worldly mindset, replace it with the TRUTH, which is the WORD of GOD. The WORD tells us that premarital sex is sin, so this is what you want to place in your mind.

Also, know that abstinence is not impossible. First, GOD would not ask you to do something you cannot do. The WORD also tells us that all things are possible with GOD. If HE wants you to abstain from sex until marriage, HE will help you to do so. After all, HE is able to do all things. This ought to be your mindset concerning premarital sex. Let go of the idea that it's not sin or that it's impossible.

Now that you've made a decision to abstain from premarital sex, you may think it's okay to date whoever you wish to date as long as you're careful. This is not true and is therefore a mindset you must let go of.

2 Corinthians 6:14 KJV
Be ye not unequally yoked together with unbelievers: for what fellowship hath righteousness with unrighteousness? and what communion hath light with darkness?

GOD wants to be the center of your marriage, and this is impossible if you marry an unbeliever. HE will not send you an unbeliever as your spouse. You should only date for the purpose of getting married. If the person doesn't seem like a likely candidate, then there is no need to proceed with that relationship.

You must understand that one conversation can lead to many things. So, what you think is a harmless date can lead to a full relationship. Once emotions are involved, it is difficult to walk away. Then, you'd find yourself outside of GOD'S will because you'd be in a relationship HE doesn't approve of.

You may also want to ask yourself what intentions an unbeliever has concerning you. You are living purely single, and this means you are waiting on GOD for your mate. Let's just say you went on that innocent date already. Do you think the person will share the same views you have of being purely single? Will the person respect those views or persuade you to sin with him or her? You may have honorable intentions, but if the other person doesn't have those same convictions, your intentions are irrelevant.

Therefore, let go of the mindset that causes you to feel that it's okay to date just anyone as long as you're careful. In truth, going on a date with a counterfeit is nothing but carelessness.

Instead, take on the mindset that you're dating with a purpose, and that purpose is marriage. So anyone who doesn't seem like a likely candidate should not get any of your time. Also, take on the mindset of not wanting to be unequally yoked.

In order to be successful in your purely single journey, you must stop viewing your single status as a punishment. This is not true at all. Single living is seasonal and should not be treated as an affliction. This kind of thinking is dangerous because anytime you see your relationship status as a problem, you will opt to choose your own mate instead of allowing GOD to choose for you. A person who is anxious to get married tends to have his or her judgment clouded when choosing a mate. Instead of hating your singleness, view it as a time for preparation. That way, you can have something to look forward to (marriage), and something to keep you busy in the meantime (mental preparation). A positive mindset is a healthier approach to being single.

Another mindset that has to be removed is being extremely emotional. Indeed, we are emotional beings, but we should not make decisions based on our emotions because our emotions can mislead us. An example of being led by emotions is seeking revenge when you feel you've been wronged. This is not pleasing to GOD. The WORD tells us that GOD will repay. Sometimes, emotions can cause us to lash out or say mean things to a loved one. The following story is an illustration of how this happens:

You are married to a great man who loves you. You come home from work after having a rough day. Your husband did not work today, and you can tell he has been home all day. The house is pretty much in disarray because none of the chores were done. You want to wind down, but you are a little irritated because you need to clean up the house first.

You find your husband in bed. *The nerve of him!* He has been lounging around all day while you were working, and he's left a mess for you to pick up. You decide to greet him, and he mumbles his response. You can't even make out what he is saying. He doesn't even get up to greet you like he always does but remains stretched out on the bed. You tell him that you've had a pretty difficult day, but he offers no feedback. His back is to you, and he doesn't turn around to acknowledge the fact that you are speaking to him. At one point in time, he was very attentive of you, but nowadays, he is so comfortable that he doesn't try anymore. You reason with yourself that he must be having an affair. That's usually why they (men) become disinterested.

Then he does the unthinkable: He asks you to get him something to drink. That's it!
You fire off with, "I know you did not just ask me to get you some water! I just got home from working my behind off, only to come home to clean up behind you. Then, you ignore me while I'm trying to talk to you, and to add insult to injury, you have the nerve to ask me to do something for you. What happened to you? I don't recognize the man I married. You were never lazy or unappreciative before. Go get it

46

yourself, or better yet, go call your other woman to go get it for you!"

He just looks at you in disbelief and says, "I didn't hear you. I'm sorry."
He gets up, grabs his drink, and leaves you with your thoughts. You tell yourself that he deserved it, and you are not about to let him walk all over you.

The world says that this is the normal reaction. You may justify it with the idea that your husband must be cheating; if not, he was still wrong. This is the world's way of handling problems and definitely an example of letting emotions get in the way. The way you treat your husband should honor GOD. So, that means you show him love whether you believe he deserves it or not. I know that it is hard to be loving when someone is acting unlovable, but it is GOD'S will. Do you think that GOD would be pleased by you disrespecting and belittling his son? If he is wrong, hand him over to GOD to deal with, and keep honoring your vows and your FATHER.

What if I told you that there is a scenario where the husband was not wrong? I actually had a similar situation happen to me.

Going back to the story, consider this: As it turns out, your husband was home all day because he wasn't feeling well. He had a really bad cold and an ear infection. This is the reason he was in bed all day. When he was mumbling unintelligibly, he was trying to tell you about his condition. He was in a lot of pain and was drowsy, and that's why his speech was incoherent. When you told him about your day, he honestly didn't hear you, and that's why he didn't respond. Remember his back was to you, so in addition to not hearing you, he didn't see you. He asked for a drink because he was too drowsy and didn't have the energy to get it himself.

Instead of being emotional, it is better to be rational, and that way, situations like this can be avoided. For this reason, being extremely emotional and treating people how you think they "deserve to be treated" needs to be removed. Replace it with the mindset of unconditional love.

Aside from wrongful mindsets, you may have to let go of some of your friends in order to walk in purity. You may have some unsaved individuals or carnal Christians for friends. They may not understand your decision to remain pure and ridicule you because of it. They may act as a stumbling block by leading you into situations where you are tempted to go outside of GOD'S will. Remember, the world does not understand righteousness and has no desire to live it. Your friends may think you're unrealistic and will probably tell you your standards are too high.

Just know that if GOD removes your friends or asks you to let go of them, it is for your good. Remember, during your singleness, you are being prepared for marriage. Your friends may be the very ones to create problems, get jealous, or possibly come between you and your spouse. GOD knows all things, but we don't know anything outside of HIM. HE has our best interest in mind anytime HE moves on our behalf.

You may have to give up your current relationship. If GOD is convicting you to live purely single, but you are in a relationship, the person you are in a relationship with may not be meant to be a part of that journey. He or she may be a stumbling block. It is likely that HE will convict you to walk away from that relationship because that person was never ordained to be your spouse. It is important for you to be able to let go of any relationship that causes you to sin.

You may have to give up a certain way of living in order to be successful at being purely single. There may be certain environments you are used to being a part of, and these environments can make the journey tougher. If you like to frequent clubs or parties, you are likely to run into counterfeits. These environments are not where you would find like-minded people, whether you are meeting with people for the purpose of courting or trying to make friends. Clubs and parties can be environments that lead you into temptation, especially during seasons when you are feeling vulnerable because of loneliness.

To maintain a purely single lifestyle, consider avoiding television shows and music that encourages you to sin. Many television shows glorify and encourage premarital sex, adultery, and promiscuity, in addition to other ungodly behaviors. If you're not careful, you can become desensitized.

Whatever you allow yourself to hear or see slowly becomes a part of you. Seeds are being planted every time you open your eyes and ears, and those seeds will grow. This is why you don't notice the effects immediately. It takes time for the seed to be watered and nurtured, but every seed in you will eventually blossom. If you keep hearing the WORD, you will be transformed by the renewing of your mind as the WORD takes root in your heart. This transformation is a process, but the process changes you as you come into agreement with the WORD of GOD. The same applies for watching television or listening to music. If you see and hear enough lust-filled content, you will become desensitized towards the sexual content. Without the WORD to counter those seeds, you will find yourself justifying certain scenarios that go against the WORD. After you become a compromising Christian, the enemy can easily trap you by causing a similar scenario to come up in your life, and you could end up justifying your own compromising actions.

Another way television and music can affect your purely single walk is by causing some of the feelings you already have within you to intensify. If you're already feeling down because you're lonely, or if you're struggling with lust, you have to be careful about what you watch or listen to. A romantic movie, book, or love song will only make feelings of loneliness worse. This makes you vulnerable and more likely to entertain a counterfeit. Also, a movie, book, or song that is sexual will intensify your desire to engage in sexual activity. Lust is hard to fight, and it often clouds people's judgment. When you're vulnerable, it is easier for you to fall into temptation than it is for you to remain pure. Sometimes, what may seem like something harmless, can be the very thing that leads to destruction. Therefore, you should exercise wisdom and use discernment in order to identify the things you may need to let go of.

Chapter 4

Acceptance

An important key to being successful in your purely single walk is accepting your current circumstances. You may not want to be single, but since you are, enjoy your season of singleness. Your circumstances will change in GOD'S timing, and HIS timing is perfect timing. Just know that if you're single, GOD wants you to be single

Be Still

While single, be still and let GOD do what HE will. Don't try to force or rush things because you may be going against GOD'S will for you, and this can only frustrate the situation further. Instead, know that things will change at the right time, and you won't have to do anything unless GOD instructs you otherwise.

Acceptance

Just because you're supposed to be single now doesn't mean you'll stay that way. You're being prepared for marriage, but not just any marriage, a GOD-centered one.

Think of preparing for marriage like preparing for a marathon. Just because you want to run a marathon doesn't make you ready or qualified to run it. You will need to train in order to prepare. How hard you have to train depends on your physical fitness, motivation, discipline, commitment to train and overall health. If you've always been physically inactive, the training itself will be difficult, since you'd be pushing your body to do something it's not used to doing. Your body would have to get used to strenuous activity, and after it did, it would eventually cooperate. Motivation, discipline, and commitment are also necessary character strengths you'd need to push you through those moments you didn't feel like training. As you can see, preparation is necessary for running a marathon.

This is how it is with marriage too. Desiring to

56

be married is not enough; you have to be prepared. If you want a marriage that is pleasing to GOD, HE must prepare you. The amount of preparation needed is dependent on your spiritual maturity, understanding, determination, commitment, and motivation. GOD has to make sure HE can trust you to build up the person HE is sending you. HE needs to know HE can entrust you with that person's heart. So, HE prepares you and your mate to have a healthy, loving marriage that brings glory to HIM. Keep in mind, you are not waiting in vain but are being prepared so that when you do marry, it will be right.

Seek GOD

When you find yourself anxious about getting married or overwhelmed by feelings of loneliness, you should take a moment to seek GOD. Spend time in worship, prayer, reading the WORD, or however the Holy Spirit leads you. Just get in HIS presence.

The beauty in being in GOD'S presence is that you'll find everything you need, including things you don't know you need. GOD is everything you need, and when you get in HIS presence, you'll find that HE'S more than enough. You'll find that loneliness won't weigh you down as much when you put your focus on GOD.

Sometimes, if the loneliness doesn't subside, you may need to go on a fast. A fast is when you deny the flesh in order to make your spirit stronger. When people fast, they deny themselves many things, but the most common fast is food fasting. The reason a fast is effective is because the flesh wants to please itself, while the spirit wants to please GOD. The flesh wars against the Spirit, and as long as we keep feeding the flesh by eating and doing other things we enjoy, the flesh gets stronger. The flesh wants to rule your actions, so going on a fast is always essential. When you fast, you cause the flesh to get weak, but remember, the second part to the fast is to make your spirit stronger. You do that by studying the WORD, spending time in prayer, and worshipping GOD. The flesh will be unable to rule, since your spirit is strong enough to overpower it.

A weak spirit can cause feelings of loneliness. Your spirit is longing for GOD, and the best remedy is to fast. The loneliness comes from your spirit longing for fellowship with the FATHER. Unfortunately, many people never learn this truth, so they never satisfy that longing. As a result, many try to satisfy their feelings of loneliness with the false security found in relationships. This often results in toxic relationships. So, fasting may be necessary since it weakens the flesh and strengthens the spirit. Therefore, any vulnerability you may be experiencing due to loneliness or lust can be overcome.

Whenever I feel led to fast, GOD shows me what I need to do to get closer to HIM. I often fast when I really have something serious I need answers for. When I get in HIS presence, it feels like reuniting with an old friend and catching up. The funny thing is: I was going to church at least four times a week, singing on the worship team, starting my own ministry, praying, and doing devotion daily. I didn't know I would miss HIM so much, but I found that the acts of worship cannot replace time spent in HIS presence. This shows how easy it is to make GOD part of your routine while getting further and further away from HIM spiritually. I used to find myself fasting for something I thought I needed, but I actually needed GOD. Each time, HE knew that I needed HIM, so HE placed a need in my heart to fast. After the fast, it became evident that what I thought I needed was irrelevant. Therefore, understand that the feelings of loneliness will become a non-factor as you try to build intimacy with the FATHER.

Whether you're fasting or not, being in GOD'S presence is beneficial to your purely single journey because it helps you to discern HIS will for your life. There may be some things or people in your life that HE may want to bring to your attention. These things and people may be distractions that are hindering your growth in HIM. Whatever the case, you can never go wrong with being in GOD'S presence. HE will always give you just what you need.

Acceptance

In order to be successful at accepting your singleness, it's good to surround yourself with like-minded people. It will be difficult for you to embrace being single if everyone in your circle is married or dating. It isn't necessary to disassociate from your friends or loved ones just because they are not single, but it would be wise to add people to your circle who are on the same journey as you. It is always good to have people who agree with you and your goals. They can encourage and pray with you too. You don't have to walk this journey alone. So, be sure to surround yourself with like-minded, optimistic people who are practicing the same lifestyle and beliefs as you are. They will hold you accountable and pray for GOD'S will in your life. Be sure to allow the Holy Spirit to lead you as you choose who to add, remove, or keep in your circle.

Chapter 5

Healing

Toxic Relationships

When people think about healing, they often think of sickness and disease, but emotional healing sometimes gets ignored. One of the consequences of choosing our own mates is finding ourselves in toxic relationships. Anyone who has been in a toxic relationship is in need of emotional healing. You will not be able to maintain a healthy, stable relationship until you are made whole.

A toxic relationship is a relationship that leaves one or both parties involved with drastic, life-altering scars after the relationship has ended. This is why GOD wants us to wait on HIM. HE wants to protect our hearts and lives from toxic relationships. Toxic relationships require so much intervention. There are soul ties that need to be severed and a great bit of deliverance is necessary. Many times, traumatic events take place, and lives are forever changed. Some life-altering situations that plague a woman long after the breakup include: the scars from abuse, unplanned pregnancies, and sexually transmitted diseases.

Domestic violence is so common that it doesn't surprise people anymore. This is alarming because many don't take the measures necessary to heal, since abuse is common. As a result, a broken woman usually goes from one relationship to the next. She leaves each relationship in a state of brokenness far worse than she was in when she entered into that relationship. This is true, even if she is never battered again. She doesn't realize she has to heal in order to be a blessing to any man. A man who stays with a woman who is in a broken state is dealing with his own issues and is in need of deliverance himself. This is because a man who is whole would recognize her brokenness and know a relationship with her wouldn't work until she's healed. Either way, a relationship with a broken woman is destined to fail, and she will be left with feelings of rejection (if she doesn't already have those feelings). Each relationship she enters will add a new scar that's in need of healing, or they will intensify existing issues that she's battling. Unless she recognizes her need for healing and takes the necessary action of being made whole again in the LORD, she will continue to repeat an ongoing cycle.

Another life-altering situation arising from toxic relationships is unplanned pregnancies, and when this happens, many turn to abortion as a solution. Abortion is so common that it is treated as another form of birth control. It is easy for a carnal-minded man to tell a woman that he is not ready for a child, but every woman who aborts a child quickly learns that there are emotional scars that come with having abortions. They usually carry that hurt by themselves, while the man moves on with his life.

I was blessed to have children, but there are many women who are unable to have children after having abortions. There are some I know personally.

Another painful result of toxic relationships is sexually transmitted diseases. Sexually transmitted diseases aren't talked about much because of the shame associated with them. Sexually transmitted diseases are real, and many who have been infected with them aren't aware of their conditions. Oftentimes, one of the parties involved in the relationship entered into the relationship with STDs; all the same, there are times that these diseases are contracted during acts of infidelity. These are serious consequences that some have to live with for the rest of their lives.

Toxic relationships always result in the need for healing for both parties involved. GOD is able and willing to heal you if you allow HIM to. Toxic relationships are prime examples of why we should wait on GOD. If we are being led by the Holy Spirit, we will pick up on the signs that we are entering toxic relationships before becoming so emotionally invested in them. GOD knows our maturity, and also, the broken areas that are hidden, even from ourselves. HE will not send us what HE knows we are not prepared for, and HE will not send us anything or anyone that is bad for us. Wait on GOD so you can avoid toxic relationships. Even though we get healed, some scars last a lifetime. Either way, HE gives us grace to get through each day.

Forgive Others

Another necessary step for healing is forgiveness. You may feel as though the person's offense is so despicable that it is unforgivable, but understand that forgiveness is for you. You are not holding the other person prisoner, but rather, you are holding yourself captive when you choose not to forgive. Forgiveness is a choice, and should not be a decision made based on your emotions,

I realize emotions are hard to control, but when you have a better idea of who your real enemy is, it will be easier to forgive those who hurt you. First, understand that a person can either be a child of the devil or a child of GOD. When you accept CHRIST into your life and obey HIM, you are adopted by the FATHER. In contrast, when you're in the world, you are obeying the prince of the world, and that makes him your father. There is no in between; you're serving either one or the other.

John 8:42-44 KJV
Jesus said unto them, If God were your Father, ye would love me: for I proceeded forth and came from God; neither came I of myself, but he sent me. Why do ye not understand my speech? Even because ye cannot hear my word. Ye are of your father the devil, and the lusts of your father ye will do. He was a murderer from the beginning, and abode not in the truth, because there is no truth in him. When he speaketh a lie, he speaketh of his own: for he is a liar, and the father of it.

Jesus was saying that those who were not

receiving the TRUTH didn't receive because they were of the devil.

The devil attempts to control both GOD'S children and his own. It is easier for him to control those who are his already, but the children of GOD fall into temptation and sin too. His agenda is to bring us to hell with him, and he'll bring as many as he can. This is the reason he uses unsaved people in our lives, or he seduces us into allowing unsaved people (his children) into our lives. That way, if he can't get to us, he'll use those closest to us to lead us into sin. Sometimes, we're led into sin by means of seduction or temptation, but he also uses strife so that we can get angry and hold on to unforgiveness. Notice that those closest to you tend to irritate you more than others. They can also be the most influential. This is why being unequally yoked is dangerous. While you cannot choose blood relatives, you can choose your friends and mate. The devil already has family members, co-workers, employers, and others in your circle on assignment to destroy you. Choosing friends or a mate on demonic assignment makes your battle harder, especially when you are emotionally attached.

The unbeliever cannot fight against the devil because the unbeliever is unaware that he or she is being attacked or that the attack is spiritual. Even if the unbeliever recognizes that he or she is being attacked, the unbeliever is unequipped for battle.

2 Corinthians 10:4 KJV
For the weapons of our warfare are not carnal, but mighty through God to the pulling down of strong holds.

People who don't have GOD in their lives will not know how to fight the devil. They are vulnerable to his tactics. The devil already has them, so it's you, the child of GOD, that he wants. When they hurt you, their father is working through them. Once you're able to separate the person from the devil influencing them, you can deal with them in love and compassion, and not as an enemy. They are in need of prayer and deliverance, and being angry with them won't make their mindsets better. Understanding who your real enemy is makes forgiveness easier.

If your healing is not enough to convince you to forgive, please know that being unforgiving is sin.

Matthew 6:14-15 KJV
For if ye forgive men their trespasses, your heavenly Father will also forgive you: But if ye forgive not men their trespasses, neither will your Father forgive your trespasses.

It is not just GOD'S will for you to forgive others, but it's GOD'S command that you forgive others. It's beneficial for you to forgive others because you need to forgive so you can heal.

Forgive Yourself
Another important person to forgive is yourself. You cannot receive healing if you have not forgiven yourself. Remember, forgiveness

should not be based on emotions. Just make a decision to forgive yourself and do it. You don't have to continuously punish yourself for mistakes that you have made.

We've already established that unforgiveness is sin. That includes not forgiving yourself too, not just others. Sin leaves a door wide open for the devil to come in. He will come in and try to make you feel condemnation. If that happens, you'll start wondering if GOD is mad at you. This can lead you into rebellion against GOD because you'll believe that you're unable to please HIM, causing you to rebel against HIM. Remember, the devil is a liar. Do not believe anything the enemy tells you. He wants you to give up on GOD and live destructively, thus causing you to forfeit your healing. Forgive yourself so you can heal properly.

Know That GOD Forgives You
Once you can accept the fact that GOD forgives you, forgiving yourself becomes easier. It doesn't matter what you did or how terrible the mistake is that you've made, if you

are genuinely sorry and don't intend to do it again, HE forgives you.

1 John 1:9 KJV
If we confess our sins, he is faithful and just to forgive us our sins, and to cleanse us from all unrighteousness.

Not only does GOD forgive your sins, but HE forgets them. HE is not like man. Even if we forgive, we don't forget the offense.

Isaiah 43:25 KJV
I, even I, am he that blotteth out thy transgressions for mine own sake, and will not remember thy sins.

Hebrews 8:12 KJV
For I will be merciful to their unrighteousness, and their sins and their iniquities will I remember no more.

Hebrews 10:17 KJV
And their sins and iniquities will I remember no more.

HE also removes our sins.

Psalms 103:12 KJV
As far as the east is from the west, so far
hath he removed our transgressions from
us.

If GOD forgives you, then you should forgive yourself. Notice that the scriptures I mentioned concerning HIS forgiveness do not specify what sins are forgiven; therefore, there is no need to worry yourself about how many mistakes you've made or how bad they were. HE forgives, forgets, and removes them. As a matter of fact, they will be used for your good. It could be for a testimony or however GOD chooses to use them.

Romans 8:28 KJV
And we know that all things work together
for good to them that love God, to them
who are the called according to his
purpose.

This has also been my experience. I have

made some mistakes that have changed my life forever. GOD forgave me, healed me, and restored me. Now, my mistakes are being used for HIS glory. I have an assignment to spread the movement of purely single living, and how to live it. My mistakes allow me to be able to relate to those who struggle, because I wasn't always living a purely single lifestyle. My story can be used as an example that people from all walks of life can relate to.

The mistakes you may feel are so big that they can't be forgiven may be the very ones to set the platform for your calling. GOD forgives you, so receive it and then forgive yourself. The healing will follow.

Soul Ties

One common form of healing needed from being in toxic relationships is deliverance from soul ties. Soul ties are common but are rarely addressed. A soul tie is an attachment that happens in the spiritual realm as well as earthly realm. There are healthy soul ties, but we will be focusing on the ungodly soul ties.

Ungodly soul ties are not hard to recognize if you take the time to look. However, it can go unnoticed if you are uninformed or unsuspecting.

The evidence that you're in a soul tie with someone includes, but is not limited to:
- When your connection to that person is so strong that it keeps you from focusing.
- You feel that you'd prefer to die or harm yourself if you can't have that person in your life.
- You can't refuse that person's requests, even if they are unreasonable or dangerous.

You cannot have an ungodly soul tie and not sin against GOD. This is because when you have an ungodly soul tie, you are controlled by the enemy.

One of the most commonly known soul ties is a tie between two people who have had premarital sex with each other. By means of fornication or adultery, that illegal union opened a door for the enemy to come in. When two people are joined in the flesh, they become one in the spiritual realm. In other words, they are joined as husband and wife. When it is ordained by GOD, it is blessed, but when it is done outside of HIS will, it is sin. You can also be soul tied to friends, your parents, or your children.

When you are soul tied, even if it is obvious that the relationship is unhealthy and, in some cases, dangerous, you cannot walk away in your own strength. The connection is too deep and requires spiritual intervention.

This is why GOD warns against being unequally yoked with unbelievers. Soul ties are difficult to break, but they can be broken with lots of prayer, denouncing, and renouncing. Healing is absolutely necessary in order to be purely single. You cannot be purely single if you're soul tied because you are in a relationship that the devil controls. In addition, you cannot have a GOD-centered marriage if you're in a soul tie with someone else. If you're soul tied to another person through sexual relations, you are still married to that person in the spiritual realm. GOD is a GOD of order, and HE will not release you to be married until you have divorced the devil and his demons.

Purely single living helps protect against soul ties because you'll avoid engaging in sex outside of the protection of a GOD-ordained marriage. Purity also protects against soul ties because you are waiting on your GOD-ordained mate, instead of entertaining counterfeits. Because sex isn't the only way you can get into a soul tie with someone, it is imperative that you don't entertain a counterfeit as soon as you recognize that he or she is a counterfeit. One seemingly harmless date or conversation can result in a soul tie. Soul ties are what makes toxic relationships last, because a person who is soul tied to another person cannot leave that person easily. Before justifying going on a date or entertaining a phone call, ask yourself if it's worth an unplanned pregnancy, being a single parent, contracting a sexually transmitted disease, or suffering through any of the consequences toxic relationships bring.

Now that you recognize how not waiting on GOD can get you into relationships that leave you broken, it's time to figure out how to heal. GOD is able to heal any hurt that you have. Sometimes praying and getting in HIS presence is enough, but there are times when more extreme measures need to be taken. You may need to fast or get outside help from your pastor or deliverance minister. For some, deliverance can be almost immediate. For others, deliverance can be a series of counseling sessions, and these sessions may take months or years. The important thing is to recognize the need for healing and to take the necessary steps to get healed.

Chapter 6

Waiting in the LORD

Now that you know GOD wants you single, you've made a decision to live a purely single life, and you've allowed GOD to heal you, it's time to wait on GOD'S timing.

Get Lost in HIM

Take all the energy and love you desire to put into a relationship and give it to GOD. There is no better way to show HIM how much HE means to you than to worship HIM. Take time to have private worship. As you worship HIM, you will develop an intimacy with HIM. You will find that you want more of HIM. You will indeed get lost in HIM.

Go on a date, not with a counterfeit, but with GOD. Pick a time that will be devoted to HIM, and you can spend it talking to HIM- not praying, but talking. Prayer is vital to your faith, and we need it like the air we breathe. However, there is a certain formality we tend to speak that is not as intimate as when we're just having a normal conversation. Try talking to GOD like you would your closest friend. Tell HIM how you feel about life, your singleness, your day, your fears, your frustrations, and whatever else you find in your heart. At least you won't have to worry about being gossiped about or judged by GOD. Your secrets are safe with HIM. Also, you'll be surprised at how much clarity you'll gain after speaking with HIM.

You can also sit quietly and study the WORD. There is so much to learn, and you'll never learn everything, so you can't get bored from monotony. The WORD of GOD is alive, and you can read the same scripture one thousand times and still get something new each time.

Things to Do

When you are spending time in GOD'S presence, HE may reveal to you your gifts, assignments, and things that need changing in your life, or HE may reveal your purpose to you. This is helpful because you don't have to be idle while waiting on your mate. HE will give you things to do in preparation for marriage and your purpose.

I came up with a to-do list so that you can be productive while waiting on your mate. You may add to the list according to your own circumstances, as long as anything you do, you do in the LORD.

1. Get before GOD. It is essential that you remain in prayer always. Get closer to GOD, and HE will reveal some of HIS plans and purpose for you. HE will bring clarity to things in your life. Also, in HIS presence, you cannot feel alone. You will feel HIS love, and it will be more than enough to fill your every need.

2. Get to know you. You may discover hidden talents or things you never knew you liked because you've never tried them. Find out what motivates you and relaxes you. What are your likes and dislikes? These things are not only important, but they are also helpful when your

special someone does come around. It makes it easier to effectively communicate what you like or don't like. For example, a man may buy a woman flowers to show his love, but she cannot stand the smell of flowers. She never realized how much she hated the smell of flowers because no one has ever bought her flowers. Because her disdain for flowers was something she was unaware of, she was unable to communicate that fact with her new friend. Use this time of singleness to get to know yourself better.

3. Now that you know you, learn to love you. Take yourself out. Go to dinner at your favorite restaurant, or go to the beach. Whatever it is that you love to do, do it without the company of others. Get off the phone sometimes. Go somewhere and don't invite your best friend. Every once in a while enjoy your own company. If you don't like to be around you, how can you want someone else to?

4. Write a book. Have you been through some challenges and overcome them? Do you have

a creative imagination? Do you know how to do something unique that many people cannot master? Write a book on that topic. You don't have to publish that book unless you want to. You may just discover that you have a hidden talent.

5. Start a business. This may seem outlandish, but why not? It doesn't have to be a huge deal. If you like to do something, and you do it well, why not get paid to do it? You may discover you have an entrepreneurial talent too.

For example, I love to sing. Some of my friends know that I love to sing, so they hire me to sing in their weddings. I get to do what I love and witness GOD'S blessing in their lives too; all the while, getting paid to do it. I don't promote or advertise that I sing, but I take a job whenever it's offered. On the other hand, I have a gift of writing and am launching my own business doing that. This is another way to discover hidden talents and be productive.

6. Get healthy. You have been thinking about

changing your diet and exercising more, so now is the time to do it! Focus on getting fit. This way, you will have a new focus.

7. Fix your credit. You probably have wanted to improve your credit score. Take the time to see what you can do and start working on it.

8. Volunteer. If you have time to feel alone, spend that time giving back in your community. Find an organization that you are passionate about, and volunteer your time there. Be a mentor, feed the homeless, or pray for the sick; the list is endless. Volunteering will keep you busy, and you'll feel great making a difference.

9. Go to school. Go get that degree! Going to school won't get any easier once you're married, so do it now! Take that writing course, learn a language, learn to play an instrument, or take art classes; again, the list is endless. You don't have to go to college for four years, but you can take a class that will give you a competitive edge on your career or business.

10. Join a small group at church. Many churches offer groups of like-minded people who get together and fellowship. Some of them do both bible study and social events. Having fellowship with the brethren helps strengthen your faith. Be wise about the time spent around others, especially married couples. While it is great to be in the presence of those who have a Godly marriage, don't overdo it. It will probably make the feelings of loneliness worse, since you are longing to have what they have. Rather, consider joining a group of singles, as they will be more understanding of your struggle. You can also encourage each other.

Of course, these are just a few of the things you can do; there are many other things you can do that will keep you productive while you wait for marriage. Remember, the Holy Spirit is your guide. Make sure any decision you make is Spirit-led, and be sensitive to GOD'S timing. Everyone's journey is unique, but GOD is glorified in them all.

A Wonderful Secret

Be patient and wait on GOD'S will. If you're a woman, GOD will send a man to you who knows your worth. You are not to do the pursuing. Pursuing men makes women appear anxious and desperate, and men can sense their impatience and use it to their advantage. The key is to understand that men are not just going along with marriage or being tricked into marriage (that may be the case in some situations), but they actually desire marriage and the benefits of marriage as well. Marriage is not some wonderful secret that only women understand and men are oblivious to. Women should keep the following in mind about men concerning marriage:

- Men pursue their mates.
- Women were created as a help mate for men.
- Women are men's gifts from GOD.

Men do the pursuing, and they have been pursuing women for ages. A man does not pursue something he does not want. For centuries, men have been known to woo the women they desire. Men do things such as buy flowers, write poetry, ask the woman's family for her hand in marriage, and many other romantic gestures designed to win over the women they are interested in. I am not saying every man has honorable intentions, so you must use discernment. The point is that men do most of the pursuing, so finding love is meaningful to them as well. There is no need to be anxious.

Another thing to keep in mind is that Eve was created because GOD didn't think Adam should be alone (Genesis 2:18). Adam was in the Garden and needed help; therefore, GOD created Eve to help him and be his wife. They weren't created at the same time, but GOD created a man and saw that the man NEEDED a mate. When Adam saw Eve, he knew that she was his wife. He didn't say, "No thanks, I think I can do this by myself," or "GOD, can you create another one? Just make her a little thinner and taller, please." Eve was just what Adam NEEDED. So, women, please know that GOD has a husband for you, and he will recognize you when he finds you.

We should also think of ourselves as a gift from GOD.

Proverbs 18:22 KJV
He who finds a wife finds what is good and receives favor from the Lord

Notice the word "find". The word "find" indicates a pursuit has taken place. The wife doesn't do the chasing; the man does. Also, when he finds a wife, he finds something good. It doesn't stop there. He receives favor from the Lord. Apparently, a wife isn't easy to come by, and a man who finds one is perceived to be favored by GOD. So, if men perceive you as treasure, then you should also see yourself as a treasure. Remember, treasure is always sought after. Therefore, women aren't the only ones who perceive marriage to be a blessing.

Don't be so anxious for marriage. Anxiousness leads to irrational and unwise decisions. There are men out there who understand a woman's worth, so don't settle because you think you are missing out. GOD is working on someone who NEEDS you. While you wait on him, keep working on being the best you (with GOD'S help, of course) that you can be. Your husband will find you because what GOD has for you is for you.

Part of purely single living is waiting on your GOD-ordained mate. You can attain this by seeking GOD, focusing on HIM, and completing the assignments HE has given you. Also, know that you are not alone in your desire for a mate. The same way you're praying and waiting, your mate is praying and waiting. You'll be a blessing to each other as GOD prepares you both to live in harmony with HIM.

Chapter 7

Why It Didn't Work

If you've made a decision to live a purely single lifestyle, you've likely made that decision because relationships your own way didn't work. You may have gotten tired of the same disappointing results and know you need to try something different. Doing life GOD'S way is not only different, but it's the best way. There are many reasons that your previous relationships didn't work, and they include: disobedience, being unequally yoked with unbelievers, and allowing sin to enter the relationship.

Disobedience

When you are a child of GOD, you have a hedge of protection around you. The devil can get close, but he cannot destroy you. When you fall outside of GOD'S will, you fall out of that protection or covering. The devil is always lurking, looking for ways to get to you. He will not miss an opportunity to catch you uncovered.

The devil is so determined that he will try to come in illegally (try to bypass your covering). This is the same way a burglar breaks into a house. He has gained access illegally because he wasn't invited in. If the homeowner is unaware, the thief may help himself to anything he wants. If the homeowner is aware, he must defend his home. He can either arm himself and fight or call the authorities. That's how the devil operates. When he thinks you're not paying attention, he will try to sneak in. That's why it is imperative that you remain alert, so you can catch him and get him off your property. He is hoping that you won't know your legal rights and power over him. He expects you to back down and let him have his way, but you have been given the power to overcome him.

Luke 10:19 KJV
Behold, I give unto you power to tread on
serpents and scorpions, and over all the
power of the enemy: and nothing shall by
any means hurt you.

The way you fight him is with the WORD.

If the devil is willing to take a chance to illegally trespass and risk you overcoming him, he definitely won't miss his chance when you come outside of GOD'S covering. An uncovered soul is easy access for him. Being disobedient to GOD gives the devil easier access to you.

If you are in a relationship that is displeasing to GOD, your relationship will go under attack because it doesn't have GOD'S covering. GOD will not bless disobedience. Disobedience is the devil's door, and through it, the enemy can come in and wreak havoc on you. He brings in strife, anger, jealousy, and anything he can use to pull you away from GOD, so he can destroy your life. Disobedience to GOD is one reason relationships don't work.

Unequally Yoked

Another reason relationships fail is when the two individuals in those relationships are unequally yoked. If you decide to pursue a relationship with an unbeliever, you can expect disaster. An unbeliever is someone who has not accepted the gospel of JESUS CHRIST. An unbeliever does not know or may not believe that JESUS died for our sins, was resurrected on the third day, and is the only way to eternal life with GOD, the FATHER. One problem with being in an unequally yoked relationship is that the relationship itself is disobedience. Remember, disobedience opens doors to the devil. Another problem with being unequally yoked is that the unbeliever is more vulnerable to the enemy's attacks and is not equipped to fight.

If a person is an unbeliever, that person is easily influenced by the devil. An unbeliever doesn't have the Holy Spirit to convict them of their wrongs. So, an unbeliever can be used by the devil to carry out assignments to destroy you. For this reason, you may meet someone with a kind heart today, and then later on, have that person display uncharacteristically mean behavior. When we study the WORD and become more like CHRIST, the unbeliever takes on more of the character of the enemy. The more you try to minister to or show kindness to an unbeliever, the nastier he or she becomes. The spirit at work in the unbeliever despises the Holy Spirit at work in you. This is why you'll often find that when you try to avoid arguments with an unbeliever, the unbeliever's attitude will often become worse towards you.

The unbeliever desires to fulfill the lusts of the flesh. Therefore, he or she is likely to give in to fornication, adultery, anger, violence, and anything to come between their relationship with you. The unbeliever will more than likely give in to temptation, and be unfaithful to you. The unbeliever will likely practice no restraint and say and do really cruel things to you for the sake of starting arguments. The devil's agenda is to pull you as far away from GOD as possible so he can make you feel worthless or cause you to seek revenge. He wants you to sin against GOD, so you can feel condemnation and continue to sin.

Your past unequally yoked relationships didn't work because the enemy was able to enter those relationships. If you try to look for an explanation in the natural realm, you will not understand what went wrong. That's because, while you're trying to keep a relationship from falling apart, the enemy is devising ways to destroy you. This is why GOD doesn't want us to be unequally yoked with unbelievers. The devil is already using the unbeliever to carry out his assignments, and you cannot have a GOD-centered marriage if the devil is controlling one or both of you.

Sin

Sin ties in every other possible reason our previous relationships didn't work. The simple definition of sin is disobedience to GOD. If we choose our own mates, fornicate, commit adultery, or do anything outside of GOD'S will, we have sinned. Sin is an open door for the enemy. When we sin against GOD, we are saying that we disagree with HIS way. This way of thinking may not be intentional, but if we are honest with ourselves, that's the statement we are making. In addition to disagreeing with GOD, we are coming into agreement with the enemy. The enemy's desire is for us to sin against GOD because when we sin, we are in the enemy's will.

Being in agreement with the enemy allows him access in the area in which you agree with him in. Allowing sin to come in the relationship is like giving the devil authority over the relationship. Once he's in, he will do what he can to destroy you. He will bring about strife, infidelity, abuse, and every form of chaos he can bring to overtake you.

Failed relationships may have left scars, shame, and uncomfortable realities that you have to live with for the rest of your life. Don't let what you can see discourage you. GOD is able and willing to forgive you, heal you, and restore you. Just understand that those relationships that brought you pain could have been worse if you had remained in them. You survived as long as you could in those relationships, but you probably would not have survived another day in them. Take the pain as a reminder of what you never want to go through again, and also, as a way to better appreciate the blessing that GOD has in store for you. Thank GOD that you're not still in a relationship that you know won't work.

Chapter 8

Think Like a Spouse

Being purely single means to wait on GOD while HE prepares us for marriage. We've already talked about how certain mindsets help us to maintain purity, but we also must understand that our minds have to be renewed concerning marriage. The goal is to have a marriage that honors GOD, so we need a Godly perspective of what a marriage entails.

Love

If you desire to be married, your definition of love has to line up with the WORD of GOD. This is the only way you can honor GOD in your marriage.

Love is a commonly misused word because it means different things to different people. There are also different kinds of love. The Bible gives us a clearer understanding of what love is. It is important to understand love so you can give pure love to others, and you can know if you are truly loved. Here are some things to keep in mind about love:

1. A person who does not know GOD cannot love you.
2. Love is a choice.
3. Love is unconditional.
4. Love is not always easy to give.

Love is a fruit of the Spirit. When you accepted CHRIST as your personal Savior, the Holy Spirit came inside you. He started convicting you of the things in you that do not please GOD. He is helping you to develop the character of CHRIST. So, a person without a personal relationship with CHRIST doesn't have the Holy Spirit teaching him or her how to love. For this reason, GOD doesn't want us unequally yoked with unbelievers. If a person isn't saved, he or she cannot love you the way you need to be loved. The unbeliever simply doesn't know how to love anyone. This is the reason that when you are cheated on, disrespected, abused, and mistreated by an unbeliever, you can't take it personally. The unbeliever will cheat on the next person to come along and the one that comes after that person. The unbeliever doesn't know how to love himself. I had to learn this the hard way.

I had a relationship that ended really badly. That man really did a number on me. Just like the others before him, I thought he was the one. I was loyal and did everything I could to keep him happy, but we weren't in the LORD. I was giving him my body without the protection of marriage. I cooked, cleaned, and did everything a "good woman" was supposed to do. We were living together, but we'd never gotten married.

One day, this man looked me in my eyes and professed his love for me. What made this so memorable was the fact that we were already saying "I love you," but there was something more intense about this moment. I believed that whatever doubt I had about his intentions towards me were unmerited because this man was head over heels in love with me. I felt I had him. He went on to tell me that he would never leave me, and he had me promise to never leave him. He told me his search was over. I was elated.

Let's fast forward to a little over a year later. He was gone out of my life. He had been having an affair with another woman, and that affair started only months after his "profession" of love.

After the relationship ended, I asked the LORD how someone who loved me could do such terrible things to me. I knew I was outside of GOD'S will when we were together, but I didn't understand how I could get cut so deeply. There were times when my ex had treated me like I was his enemy, but afterward, he would tell me that he knew he would never find a woman who would do the things I did for him. He said that he didn't know why he mistreated me. That statement alone didn't make any sense to me, so I tried to get an understanding from GOD. I was not going to reconcile with him, but I was just perplexed. The LORD answered me and said that my ex couldn't love me or our child because he didn't know HIM. In fact, my ex did not love himself.

The LORD began to remind me of a conversation I'd had with my ex where he was talking about his love for alcohol. He was telling me that if he was on life support, and the doctors told him he had to stop drinking, he wanted me to just give him his vodka so he could die happy. Of course in my carnality, I thought that statement was cute.

Then I heard the Lord say, "You can't take it personally. He didn't love himself. He couldn't love you because he couldn't love at all. If he can take pride in killing his body, why would he treat you or his seed any differently?" It suddenly made sense. He wasn't an Academy Award-winning actor. He really believed what he was saying to me when he professed his "love" for me, but neither he nor I had any idea that it wasn't real. He loved me the way he could: unstable, unreliable and conditional.

That's why he was able to "fall out of love" so easily. He did not have GOD, so he was incapable of truly loving me, himself, or others.

Once you have the ability to love, you can make a decision to love, contrary to popular belief. The world paints a picture of this emotion that takes over us that we can't help but feel (and not feel), depending on the circumstances. This feeling is actually lust, infatuation, obsession, or a combination. When you look at what the Bible says about love, this statement will make more sense to you. JESUS commands us to love others. Therefore, it is a choice to love or not to love.

1 Corinthians 13:4-7 ASV
Love suffereth long, and is kind; love envieth not; love vaunteth not itself, is not puffed up, doth not behave itself unseemly, seeketh not its own, is not provoked, taketh not account of evil; rejoiceth not in unrighteousness, but rejoiceth with the truth; beareth all things, believeth all things, hopeth all things, endureth all

things.

The biblical description of love is indicative of love being a choice. You have to make a conscious effort to do the things associated with love. Things like patience don't just happen; an effort is made. Also, each characteristic requires self control and is not based on emotions.

Once you understand that love is a choice, it is easier to CHOOSE to love unconditionally. It is essential for a wife to love her husband unconditionally and vice versa. If you decide to let emotions dictate whether or not to show your spouse love, your marriage will be as unstable as your emotions. Your mind has to be renewed to give love to someone who doesn't always deserve it. Otherwise, you will tear your spouse down, rather than build him or her up whenever you're upset about something your spouse did. This love is not only conditional, but it is unfair.

As humans, we are limited in our

understandings. We can't know everything, especially the heart of man. The very thing that may cause you to become upset with your spouse could very well be a misunderstanding or something that's beyond your spouse's control. That's because your perception is only reality to you. Therefore, it is better to consistently show love, even when you don't think your spouse (or others) deserves it. After all, you could be wrong, and even if your spouse is wrong, it is better to hand him or her over to GOD while you keep honoring the FATHER by showing love.

Another thing you must accept is that it is not always easy to love someone. The true love that GOD teaches us to give to each other is a challenge that gets harder as we get closer to an individual. The ones you are closest to can be the hardest to love because they are able to hurt you worse than others can. You have to develop Godly characteristics such as patience to deal with family and close friends. Your loved ones are the people who tend to show you their true natures, and their ways aren't always pretty.

One biblical description of love that I found to be a challenge is *"keeping no record of wrong" (NIV version).* When I read that in 1 Corinthians 13, I knew that I had a lot to learn about love. I thought that I was the most loving girlfriend a man could ever have, but I had a problem letting go of the past. I was the type of girlfriend who'd remind my boyfriends of how lucky they were that I hadn't stopped loving them after all they'd put me through. I was the loving girlfriend when things were going well, but the moment a man would do something wrong, I'd remind him of how he'd always mess things up when they were going well. As hard as it was for me to face, I had to come to grips with the fact that I was a nightmare. Who would want to deal with that kind of attitude? I had to remind a man of how good of a person I was because I obviously needed to convince myself that I was good. I had to come to terms with the fact that I was battling the feeling of unworthiness and punishing boyfriends for those feelings by putting them down so I could feel worthy. I'm so glad that GOD brought those issues to my attention, because my future husband would have been miserable if I had not had a change of heart. Also, you shouldn't have to convince anyone that you are a blessing. GOD knows your worth and will give you to a mate who knows your worth. Your GOD-ordained spouse will be thanking GOD for you because you're such a blessing.

Having your mind renewed about love is definitely helpful in preparing you for marriage. Ask the Holy Spirit to show you what needs changing in you, and He will.

Trust

Trust is another area where worldly thinking can destroy a marriage. The world tells you not to trust at all if you want to have the upper hand in the relationship and avoid being hurt. Needless to say, you should not be trying to have the upper hand in anything; instead, you must give all control to GOD. You may have also heard that quote, "Without trust, a relationship cannot survive" (Author unknown).

This is true. Understand that there is no love without trust. Lack of trust will destroy a relationship, and trusting GOD will help you trust your spouse.

According to 1 Corinthians 13, love trusts. If trust is a characteristic of love, then we can conclude that one cannot have love without trust. If you desire a marriage that honors GOD, then trust is necessary. If you believe you can enter a marriage without trust, you are setting the marriage up for failure. It may be difficult to let your guard down, especially if you've been hurt before, but the marriage won't survive without trust.

Lacking trust in a marriage may cause you to partake in actions that are offensive to your spouse. If you think it is okay to go through your spouse's phone or other personal belongings, then you definitely lack trust. Your mind also has to be renewed. While a marriage is supposed to be open and without secrets, it is not okay to invade a person's privacy. Also, once you start going through his or her things, you won't stop going through them. This behavior becomes an obsession, and you won't stop until you find something. If you don't find anything, your mind will tell you that you didn't conduct a thorough search. Eventually, you will find something, and because you have a one track mind, something innocent can be blown way out of proportion. This can cause the both of you to be miserable because you are not finding what you are looking for and your spouse is irritated with your invasion of his or her privacy. No one wants to feel like they cannot be trusted. Furthermore, no one wants their things searched either. This kind of behavior destroys marriages.

The remedy is to trust GOD. Trust HIM to send you a spouse who you can trust. When you choose on your own, you may end up with a worldly person. If you marry a worldly person, you will have good reason to question his or her trustworthiness. It still doesn't justify all the detective work, but it's understandable why you may have doubts about your partner. We already know that a person who does not know

GOD cannot love anyone else and may engage in activities that may make you question his or her fidelity. Even in this case, there is no need to search through your spouse's things. GOD will reveal to you anything you NEED to know. If you allow the Holy Spirit to lead you, then whatever information that is necessary for you to know WILL FIND YOU. GOD is just that faithful. HE will protect you. However, this is one of the reasons HE doesn't want us unequally yoked with an unbeliever. You can spare yourself this type of heartache by just obeying GOD.

Trust GOD to send you your mate. HE knows the heart of man, and HE is not wicked. HE will send you exactly what you need. HE knows your heart, your struggles, your pain, and HE will send a spouse who HE can trust with your heart.

Your future spouse has to prove himself or herself worthy of having you. There is no need for detective work because even the most conniving person cannot hide ANYTHING from

GOD. If he or she is proven trustworthy by GOD, then you should trust GOD enough to trust the person HE sends to you. A true man or woman of GOD has reverence for HIM and does not desire to hurt anything or anyone who is cherished by GOD. You are cherished by GOD, and HE wants you to have a spouse who loves and fears HIM more than he or she loves you. This is why it is crucial to wait on GOD. Humans are flawed and can make mistakes, but someone who allows Christ to lead them; someone who puts GOD first and is Holy Spirit-filled, is worthy of being trusted because of what GOD is doing in them. Trust GOD to send your spouse, and HE'LL send someone HE trusts. Therefore, you can trust that person as well.

Submissiveness

Another area where worldly thinking can destroy a marriage is the willingness of a wife to submit to her husband. In a society that celebrates the "independent woman", submissiveness is discouraged. Let's be clear: CHRIST leads the husband, and the husband leads the wife. GOD has designed marriage, and HE has arranged for the wife to submit to her husband. Keep in mind that a wife being submissive to her husband is the will of GOD. Submission is not weakness, and it will bless the marriage.

CHRIST leads the husband, and the husband leads his wife. This is the order of a Godly marriage. If a woman puts her trust in GOD to send her husband, he (her husband) won't steer her wrong because he would be submitted to CHRIST. She must understand that by biblical definition, her husband being submitted to CHRIST not only means he will be heading in the right direction, but he will love her and not try to rule over her. The Bible tells wives to submit to their husbands, and the Bible commands the husband to love his wife as CHRIST loves the church. If a husband submits to Christ, he will lead his wife in a manner that brings GOD glory, and this will benefit the entire family. He will be careful not to abuse his authority, and he will cherish his blessing (the wife) from GOD.

In order for a wife to submit to her husband, she must submit to GOD. When she is submitted to GOD, she will have a desire to please HIM. Therefore, it would give her great pleasure to submit to the husband GOD sends her because her first priority is to please GOD.

A wife may find it hard to submit to her husband when she has rebellion in her heart. She is not submitted to GOD, and therefore, it is impossible for her to submit to her husband. She will oppose everything the husband does unless his choices personally benefit her. A marriage like this cannot work because a wife is supposed to be her husband's helper. How can a man realize his dreams when his wife does not believe in his GOD-given vision? Nothing is impossible for GOD, but if the husband of a non-submissive wife was to succeed in anything, it would be without his wife's blessing. This in itself creates division between the couple.

Do not be fooled; division is a plan of the enemy! Not being submitted to GOD opens a door for the enemy to come in.

James 4:7 KJV
Submit yourselves therefore to God. Resist the devil, and he will flee from you.

You can resist the devil all you want, but if your heart is not submitted to GOD, he (the enemy) will gain legal access to you because you stepped out from under GOD'S covering with your disobedience. The devil is stubborn! HE will not leave if he feels he has legal ground, and he is oftentimes stubborn about leaving when he doesn't have any legal grounds. So you want to make sure you don't leave any doors open to him. Imagine a house with no fence. It is difficult to keep trespassers off the property. In the same way, a heart not submitted to GOD is vulnerable to the enemy because there is no covering (fence) to keep him out.

On the other hand, a husband is not to abuse the authority he is given. He is in no way to control his wife at anytime. Even if he feels he has a good reason to control his wife, and even if he feels the outcome of him ruling over her would be beneficial to their marriage, he is not justified by GOD in controlling his wife.

Let's look at it this way. GOD is sovereign. HE can do anything HE pleases, including control us, but chooses not to. If GOD controlled us, no one would go to hell. There is no better reason for HIM to intervene against our will than to keep us from going to hell. HE would be justified (although HE answers to no one) in controlling us, but HE chose to give us free will. Salvation is something we willfully accept or reject, although it is HIS will that we all receive it. So what other reason can anyone have for controlling people that carries more weight than saving a soul? If GOD doesn't exercise HIS ability to control others, yet a human being feels justified in their attempt to control others, that person is doing something far worse than playing GOD. He or she is attempting to rise above GOD. Therefore, it is not GOD'S will for anyone to control another person or to manipulate the person into doing something against his or her will.

A marriage blessed by GOD is covered by HIM. That's why we say, "What GOD has joined together, let no man put asunder." That includes the devil. Make no mistake about it, the devil will try to destroy your marriage. He knows if your marriage fails, it will affect your entire family. This is why it is imperative that you renew your mind about living purely-single, rather than just attempting to live the lifestyle without a real understanding of it. If you don't understand how your mindset can set you up for failure, you won't know how to fix any problem that arises before it is too late. Being unwilling to allow GOD to prepare you to be a spouse can have a traumatic effect on your life and the lives of others.

Do not be dismayed; there is hope. You can never be too far off course to be redeemed. If you repent and submit your issues to GOD, HE can and will deliver you. Sometimes deliverance is instant and is something you can do on your own; while for some, it is a long process and they may need to be ministered to by someone with a deliverance ministry.

John 8:36 KJV
If the Son therefore shall make you free, ye shall be free indeed.

There is no issue too great for GOD to fix.

There may be other mindsets that make it difficult for a wife to submit to her husband, such as her having a misconception of what submission is. Whatever the reason, it is important for her to have a renewed mind about being submissive to her husband. If she can submit to GOD and accept that it is GOD'S desire for her to submit to her husband, her marriage has an advantage.

Another thing to keep in mind about submissiveness is that it is not weakness. It takes courage to have the kind of faith needed to submit to someone. It is also commendable to do so in a society that frowns upon this mindset. A submissive wife may stand alone in her circle of friends, even amongst other Christians. It takes courage to stand alone in your faith. There is nothing weak about being willing to be ostracized, ridiculed, persecuted, or mocked for your willingness to stand on your faith. Being submitted to her GOD-given husband also tells GOD that she (the wife) trusts HIM.

A submissive wife brings blessings to her marriage. GOD will bless her marriage because of her obedience. So, even if the husband unintentionally leads her in the wrong direction, a Godly wife will follow his lead (in the LORD), and GOD will right all wrongs because of her faith. A submissive wife is a blessing to her husband because any man of GOD would love to know that his wife has his back in everything he does (in the LORD). He is confident because he feels loved and respected. If his wife does disagree with him, he considers her thoughts because he values her and her opinion. This keeps them united and the home at peace. This is the blessing that comes when a woman of GOD is submissive to the man GOD sent to be her husband, and when the husband loves and honors his wife, instead of abusing his authority.

Patience

Patience is another fruit of the Spirit that is beneficial to a successful marriage. Living purely single is a great way to exercise patience, since you're waiting on GOD'S timing. Patience is necessary in marriage and in life. Patience is especially needed when there are disagreements between a husband and his wife. You may be tempted to give your spouse a piece of your mind when you feel wronged, but such ways are not pleasing to GOD. If your spouse possesses characteristics that make it difficult to get along with them, leave your spouse to GOD. Do not engage in offensive behavior; instead, allow GOD to handle the situation. This requires patience and helps keep the marriage peaceful.

It is wise to work on developing all the fruit of the Spirit. They are essential for life and will definitely benefit your marriage.

Chapter 9

Preparing

Purely single living is about waiting on GOD for your spouse, but what you do while you're waiting is important. Accepting your singleness, renewing your mind, and receiving healing is all about preparation. You are preparing to be a spouse in a marriage that honors GOD. This is a time to really do some self-reflecting. Get to know who you are by digging deep and uncovering those hidden parts of yourself. Preparation helps you to face whatever you uncover; especially if what you find is unpleasant.

Love Yourself

Loving yourself is one very important thing you need to make sure you learn to do. If you don't love yourself, you'll have a hard time receiving someone else's love. You'll probably question your spouse's love, and therefore, you'll be suspicious about your spouse's intentions and test him or her accordingly. Another problem with not loving yourself is that you won't be able to love others, and this can be frustrating for your spouse.

Not loving yourself also makes you likely to choose a mate who doesn't appreciate you. You may feel unworthy of true love and settle for someone who mistreats you. A person who doesn't love himself or herself is prone to toxic relationships. This low self-perception will only make the situation worse. Being mistreated could cause the person's feelings of unworthiness to intensify.

The solution to learning how to love is to develop an intimate relationship with the FATHER.

1 John 4:7-8 KJV
Beloved, let us love one another: for love is of God; and every one that loveth is born of God, and knoweth God. He that loveth not knoweth not God; for God is love.

HE will love you and show you how to love yourself. You cannot love yourself or others without knowing GOD.

1 John 4:16 KJV
And we have known and believed the love that God hath to us. God is love; and he that dwelleth in love dwelleth in God, and God in him.

As you go deeper into GOD'S presence, you will see yourself the way HE sees you, and you won't be able to help feeling special.

Completeness

The world tells us that our spouses complete us, but two incomplete people cannot make a marriage work. One complete person in a marriage is not going to work either. If you feel incomplete, you must fill that void prior to getting married; otherwise, you will place unrealistic expectations on your spouse. Completeness does not come from your spouse; it must be achieved prior to marriage.

Preparing

When a person feels incomplete, there is a void that needs filling in them. Sadly, people can spend their entire lives filling that void with things that only work temporarily. They may try to fill it with money, drugs, alcohol, sex, and companionship. Expecting your spouse to complete you is an unrealistic and unfair responsibility to put on another human being. The only person who can fill that void is JESUS. The only person who can complete you is JESUS. Don't expect a marriage to fill the void because, by doing so, you would be setting yourself up for disappointment.

Completeness should be achieved prior to marriage because when you marry a person, you also take on that person's problems. It is unfair to subject someone to the kind of burden that incompleteness brings. This can be extremely overbearing for both parties in the marriage. Therefore, if you feel incomplete, you should not think about marriage until that issue is resolved. If not, you will be more of a burden than a blessing to your spouse.

Preparing

Two people getting married should complement each other. Complementing and completing are two different things. When you complement your spouse, he or she is already whole, but you just made your spouse a better person. This means you still function independently of each other.

Let me give you an example. Some people like milk with their cookies. Milk can be a great complement for cookies because they go well together. Some people may even say milk makes the cookies better. However, the cookies would still be good without milk, and the milk can function without the cookies. They can be consumed independent of each other, but they add value to each other when consumed together. Therefore, milk and cookies are both complete without each other but better together.

This is how a healthy marriage between two complete individuals looks. Each individual has his or her own identity and functions well independent of his or her spouse. Yet, when they come together, they become something better than what they are individually. A husband and wife should be great alone but better together.

On the other hand, consider the following example: You need sugar to make a great cookie. The sugar doesn't make the cookie better but it actually makes the cookie a cookie. Needless to say, the sugar is still sugar without the cookie, but the sugar has to give up itself to make the cookie good. Yet, the cookie isn't a cookie without the sugar.

This is what a marriage looks like when one spouse is whole and the other isn't. The sugar represents the whole person, and the cookie represents the incomplete person. The whole person is independently whole, but the incomplete person needs the whole person just to feel whole. A marriage like this becomes unhealthy because one person has to give so much of themselves to their spouse, while the other spouse receives much but is unable to give much. As a result, the whole person becomes incomplete after giving so much of himself or herself and not receiving anything in return. This can be compared to a cookie that doesn't have enough sugar to be sweet. If the sugar ran out, and the cookie wasn't sweet, it would defeat the purpose of having the cookie. A couple like this does not improve the quality of life for each other; instead, they're no good together.

The sugar and cookie illustration is also representative of CHRIST in our lives. The cookie symbolizes us. Before having CHRIST, we were without an identity, but with HIM, we are filled with greatness and purpose. The thing is the sugar supply is endless. CHRIST has more than enough (sugar) to supply our needs.

In conclusion, prior to marriage, each individual must love himself or herself in order to give and receive love. Experiencing the love of GOD will eliminate the feeling of unworthiness that may cause a person to not love himself or herself. Each individual must be whole so that

the couple will complement each other, rather
than attempting to complete each other.

Chapter 10

Setting Standards

In the previous chapters, we talked about what purely single living is, how to live it, and how to prepare for a Godly marriage. Now, we will talk about purely single living while courting. Living a pure life while courting is harder than just waiting on GOD because the principles of living in purity will be put into practice. You may endure a greater temptation than you'd endured when you were alone. It is imperative that you set standards so that you can maintain your purely single lifestyle while you're with that special person.

Remember: To live purely single, you must be proactive. Singleness may or may not be a choice, but living purely single is always a choice. It goes without saying that things can happen that may tempt you to compromise your stance, but if you are prepared, you can overcome temptation. In order to be proactive, you must set standards and stick by them.

Courting versus Dating

The second part to purely single living is waiting on your GOD-ordained spouse. This means that you will only enter romantic relationships with the goal of marriage in mind. When you meet someone who is a good candidate, you begin courting that person.

Courting is different from dating, because when dating, marriage isn't always the goal. In fact, when dating, the goals are often undefined. On the other hand, courting is specifically for the purpose of marrying. The purpose of courting is to do the will of GOD by waiting on the one HE has for you and maintaining your purity. Courting is about honoring GOD through your relationship.

Before you enter into any relationship, establish that you are courting. Make sure that there is a mutual understanding that you're courting and not dating casually.

Weeding Out the Counterfeits

We've already established that if you are living purely single, you will avoid knowingly entertaining counterfeits. It is inevitable to run into counterfeits, but you must recognize a counterfeit when you see one so you can weed them out.

Making a decision to live a purely single life may eliminate some counterfeits because many people won't understand your lifestyle. However, there are people who will challenge you and have no problem pursuing you, even though they do not have the same agenda for the relationship as you do. It is good to recognize counterfeits and avoid wasting time with them.

Since men are natural predators, women are more susceptible to being pursued by counterfeits. However, a woman can be a counterfeit sent to distract a man from his purpose as well. One way a woman can weed out a counterfeit is by allowing him to speak.

James 1:19 KJV
Wherefore, my beloved brethren, let every
man be swift to hear, slow to speak, slow to
wrath.

James 1:19 is referring to being careful about
what you say when you're angry, and it is also
a good concept to apply in all areas of your life.
When selecting a life partner, you need to
make sure you really know the person, and not
just who he or she portrays himself or herself
to be.

One thing that can stand in the way of you
getting to know a potential mate is disclosing
too much about yourself too soon. People can
be deceptive; not everyone has good
intentions. Because people can be deceptive,
you have to be aware of their real agendas.
When you disclose too much about yourself
right away, it becomes easier for someone to
fool you because that person will know what to
say to get closer to you. This can cause you to
allow someone you would otherwise avoid to
get into your comfort zone. This is not only a

possible threat to your purely single walk, but it can also potentially be a threat to your safety.

Not having control over the information you disclose can put you and loved ones in danger. There are lots of evil people in this world. You could find yourself entertaining a serial killer, a thief, or a rapist. You don't want to find out that a person is a predator by becoming their prey. You can't always tell what's in a person from a few meetings and a few conversations. Some people hide their evils so well that it may take years to find out the truth. However, make sure you let the Holy Spirit guide you when allowing people in your life. He will let you know if something is wrong. Avoid letting people you are not comfortable with know things like your address, what school your children attend, the location of your place of employment, or any other compromising or identifying information. Revealing too much about yourself can cause you and your loved ones to become victims of crimes, so be sure to use discretion.

We open the door for deceit when we disclose

too much, and that's why it is good to be slow to speak and quick to listen. This is especially true for women when being approached by men. Men are natural predators, and they don't always have honorable intentions. A man will do whatever it takes to get a woman once he decides he wants that woman. Some men have no problem being deceitful, as long as it works in getting them what they want.

I often hear women say things like, "He sold me a dream." That phrase means that some man told her what she wanted to hear, even though it wasn't true. I have experienced being "sold a dream" numerous times. If you don't hastily tell a person all of your dreams, your ambitions, what your ideal mate is like, what your ex-boyfriend did to you, and everything else on your heart, he can't "sell you a dream." He would have to work harder at figuring out what makes you tick. I want to share with you an example of just how willing a man is to display what he thinks will attract you. Women are not excluded; it's just more prevalent with men, since men are usually the pursuer in relationships.

I was a junior in high school, and I'd ridden the school bus to school. At that time, I would always keep to myself. I was also more mature for my age because I was the eldest of my siblings. I'd practically raised them, and it showed. There was always a group of guys at the back of the bus horsing around, joking, and being vulgar. One of them was especially vulgar, and he was always talking loudly about the "easy girls" he had been with. He was very colorful when describing his encounters, and I was disgusted by how he carried himself.

One day, while walking home from the bus stop, he approached me. I didn't want to be bothered by him, but I let him speak anyway. He said, "Excuse me. How are you?" I was shocked that he could actually be so articulate, and I answered him by saying, "I'm fine. And you?" He proceeded to compliment me, and he politely asked me for my phone number. I respectfully declined.

Setting Standards

Even though I had never had a conversation with this guy, he observed me long enough to know how to approach me. He had studied me in his attempt to deceive me, but his flattery didn't work on me. So, imagine when you tell a deceitful man everything he needs to know about you. You are giving him the platform to build every lie he needs to tell you, instead of letting him work at figuring you out. At least when he tries to figure you out, there's a chance of him being wrong, but when you're an open book, it is easier for him to deceive you.

Be slow to speak and quick to listen when selecting a mate, so you can discern your potential mate's heart. The Word tells us that out of the heart flows the issues of life. In other words, you can see the condition of a person's heart by listening to the things that person says because we speak from the heart. People don't always say what they mean initially, but they do let it all out eventually. They need just enough time to get comfortable. When you are doing all the talking, you are making it easy for a person to hide who he or she really is, thus giving that person the opportunity to examine your heart while concealing their own. The story about the young man on my school bus is a good example of that. He didn't realize that while he was talking to his friends, he was revealing his heart to me. With his friends, he was being himself and showing his true colors, but when he approached me, he showed me a different character. He showed me his willingness to misrepresent himself in order to have a chance with me. I've heard him approach other girls with lousy pick up lines like, "Hey lil' mama," and by using other distasteful comments. So, that respectful salutation he gave me was a facade. I didn't have to investigate; he told me everything I needed to know without his knowledge. A deceitful person will always have to remove his or her mask at some point.

In conclusion, do what the Bible says, and be slow to speak and quick to listen. Apply that in every situation you find yourself in. I am not saying that you should never speak, just don't give up everything about yourself all at once. Use wisdom. You will find that this principle will keep you from endangering yourself and others. It will also make it easier to detect deception and help you to see a person's heart. Although we trust GOD to protect us, we must also exercise the wisdom HE gave us.

No Sex

Purely single living is about abstinence until marriage. Anytime you meet a potential spouse, you must make it clear to them that there will be no sex until marriage. It may seem as if I'm stating the obvious, but there needs to be clear boundaries set from the onset of a relationship. There are certain behaviors that may appear innocent, but those behaviors set the stage for you to be tempted. Setting boundaries may seem a little extreme, but you have to be proactive and not reactive to protect your purity. The dynamics of each relationship are different, so what works for one person may not necessarily work for another person. What one couple absolutely cannot overcome, another couple may have little or no trouble getting through. Just keep in mind that the goal is to honor GOD while courting and not try to see what you can get away with without actually falling. You should never gamble with your purity.

Here are a few areas where boundaries should be set.

1. **Kissing:** Kissing should be reserved for marriage. The problem with kissing is it often leads to more. A peck is okay, but deep, passionate kisses are a wide open door to sex.

2. **Groping:** Like kissing, groping body parts is only welcoming sexual arousal. It is a lot easier to prevent sex from happening than to stop the process leading to it. When sexual desires overtake you, it is extremely difficult to rationalize. When both of you want to have sex, it is even harder to stop from giving into temptation; therefore, it is wise to not start at all.

3. **Conversation:** Try to keep the

conversations clean. Before you perform any act, whether good or bad, you thought about it and acted it out in your head. If you're talking about it, you're thinking about it, and if you're thinking about it, you will likely do it.

Talking about sex and expecting it not to happen is like cooking your favorite meal, looking at it, and deciding that neither you nor anyone else can eat it. It's highly unlikely and impractical. Keep your conversations and mind holy.

4. **Time spent:** Try to avoid spending too much time alone. This is difficult because people who are attracted to each other will want to be around each other, but temptation is hard to overcome when no one else is around. It is better to go out on group dates or to places that are public.

The movies are a bad idea for many reasons. It's dark, it's an intimate environment, and you can't get to know each other because you can't talk. Also, the wrong type of movie may set the stage for temptation.

Another thing to consider is how late you plan to be out. Giving yourself a curfew may seem childish but can be very necessary. Being out at night increases the chances of having premarital sex. It is also easier to be alone at night than during the day. It is good to have an idea of how late is too late to be out. Then stick by what you decide to do.

5. **Phone conversations:** It is good to establish a time to be on the phone. Phone calls after the midnight hour often lead to conversations about sex. Needless to say, some people work late hours and are probably only available after midnight. Just be sure to be alert.

6. **Favors:** Everyone can use a little help sometimes, and it's great to have someone who doesn't mind doing favors for you, but giving too many favors or

large favors can lead to the person giving the favors feeling like he or she is owed something. For example, a man may expect sexual favors in return for giving the woman he's pursing material things. Also, the person receiving the favors may feel obligated to compromise their purity.

Another thing about giving and receiving favors is that favors often cause couples to assume spousal duties with each other. A woman may feel the need to cook, clean, and do laundry for the man she's courting. This will lead her to feeling as if she is a wife, and she will likely get comfortable enough to have premarital sex with the man she's courting. Because she feels married, she will likely begin to act married.

You should always have a conversation with any potential mate about boundaries when it comes to giving and receiving favors.

7. **Spending money:** There should be a conversation about the expectations of

each person concerning how much money is too much money spent. The same rules we discussed concerning favors apply here.

Of course, the above list displays only some of the ways you can be proactive about being purely single. The important thing is to allow the Holy Spirit to lead you and to avoid anything that leads you into temptation.

Never Settle

Once you've set standards to maintain your purity, do not compromise those standards. Never put a relationship before GOD. If living purely single is repelling all your prospects, thank GOD for HIS will. You don't want someone who isn't willing to please GOD because that person will not be a Godly spouse. The relationship would be unstable, and it would not be blessed by GOD. Keep in mind that if it doesn't work, it wasn't meant to be.

You shouldn't have to convince someone to

please GOD. If the person isn't convinced that GOD wants the two of you to walk in purity, you have nothing else to discuss. Remember, the goal is not to have just any marriage, but the goal is to have a Godly marriage.

www.ingramcontent.com/pod-product-compliance
Lightning Source LLC
Chambersburg PA
CBHW072011040426
42447CB00009B/1586